Proud to be an Introvert

How Introverts Can Use their Unique Strengths to be More Successful in Life

KENNY MATTHEWS

Legal & Disclaimer

Upon using the contents and information contained in this book, you agree to hold harmless the Author from and against any damages, costs, and expenses, including any legal fees potentially resulting from the application of any of the information provided by this book. This disclaimer applies to any loss, damages or injury caused by the use and application, whether directly or indirectly, of any advice or information presented, whether for breach of contract, tort, negligence, personal injury, criminal intent, or under any other cause of action.

You agree to accept all risks of using the information presented inside this book.

You agree that by continuing to read this book, where appropriate and/or necessary, you shall consult a professional (including but not limited to your doctor, attorney, or financial advisor or such other advisor as needed) before using any of the suggested remedies, techniques, or information in this book.

Table of Contents

Introduction

Introverts are indeed an obscure lot. It's as if they come from another planet. Their attitudes may come off as out-of-this-world to the uninitiated, hence isolating introverts even further.

So the question is, what is it about introverts that make them a peculiar group? We can think of many ways to describe them, and most of them are not very pretty.

Being the outcasts and brain-dead stoic pseudo-intellectuals many people seem to peddle around, introverts are described as detached and at most, unapproachable. It is because of these traits, being an introvert has nurtured for itself a negative connotation. No one likes to go near someone who would rather sit down, read books, and discuss the Chaos Theory. Extroversion has for some reason, become something to long for. This is because extroversion is love, and extroversion is life. The people blessed with a talent to speak in front of an audience without so much as stuttering are the real heroes of the day, and those at the sidelines are nothing but dull spectators who will miss out on a lot in life.

What many don't know is that introverts are like Kinder Eggs. They may look like harmless plastic shells, but it is what's within them that makes them so special. And this book sets out to prove introverts are more than meets the eye. It's only a matter of digging deeper into their core and tapping into their potential to be great people.

If you consider yourself to be one of what Kerouac describes as fabulous roman candles in the sky, this book will help you navigate through that powerful mind of yours and dig out that special crystal in you that makes you great.

In this vein, let me give you my warmest appreciation for purchasing this book. You know you are more than the labels people put on you, and there is a good reason for buying this book in the first place. This is because you believe in yourself as someone who in the comforts of his silence and his castle, can use his solitude to discover the great power that lies within.

By purchasing this book, you have already realized that being an introvert does not mean you should stay on the sidelines all your life. Being an introvert is something much more amazing than anyone can imagine. It is more about looking within yourself, following your passions and dreams, and striving to make every little imagination in your head into a reality. For all we know, introverts are just firecrackers waiting for that single spark of inspiration to explode into a colorful sky tapestry of creativity.

I hope by the end of this book, you will have realized the most vital strengths of an introvert. No longer will you be ashamed of being a wallflower, because you know your worth as a human being who just wants to think about how to make yourself and the world better.

Chapter 1. Deconstructing the introvert

We start by asking the question, "What makes an introvert?"

Many people have peddled the image of the weird kid. You know, that classmate of yours who does not talk much; who chooses to spend the night reading books and binge watching Big Bang Theory while, other people's idea of an awesome Saturday night is going binge drinking like there is no tomorrow. We are also drawn into the image of a geek who joins nerdy clubs, who discusses nerdy things, and who only talks to people who pretty much possess the same level of weirdness.

He is an outcast. She is a vagrant. He is a hipster. She is a loner. These people came to be known as introverts. The name itself describes the main trope of their personality: Detached and focused merely on the chaos happening within their heads. They are people who live in shells and cottages; who would rather stay away from the many dangers that make life exciting.

To other people, introverts are the ones who make parties dull. Because of their detachment from social conventions and their indifference to the fads of today, introverts are seen to be the anti-thesis of life. Instead of taking the bull by the horns, they would rather join an animal rights group. The extroverts will never understand why introverts settle for the blandest versions of life. For many, we affirm life by taking risks and going on adrenaline-pumping adventures. Introverts, well, they just want to curl up into little balls and watch the days go by with dreary eyes.

The bigger question is, why do we even bother complaining about the way introverts live their lives? For all we care, happiness depends entirely on how you want your life to turn out. It is never about doing what others think is cool or great or life-giving.

Life denying?

In this world, we are made to realize that life is too short. Which is why most people would rather spend it with their primal instincts turned on. We need to enjoy the hell out of it, or we will end up in deathbeds regretting the day we bought the ticket and took the ride (words straight from the drug-crazed pen of Hunter S. Thompson).

If that is so, we should then come to call introverts as deniers. They came into this world without thinking of leaving it high and dry. Naturally of course, happiness is a relative concept. The way we were brought up plays a major role in shaping our personalities well into adulthood. In essence, there is truth in saying introverts are made and not born, but only because they were sold the idea of introversion as a cool thing.

It is easy for many to say they are introverts only because they go to bookstores and contemplate about the cosmos over an espresso. Introversion has become a twisted concept in today's society; so misunderstood that people begin to attach certain labels to individuals with characteristics along the previously mentioned lines.

Anyone can claim to be an introvert, but only a true intellectual recluse can know the difference between faking and actually existing as the real intellectual recluse that he is.

The Real Score with Introverts

So, what makes an introvert?

Well, we could say that an introvert is someone who would rather see the world from another perspective. People fall into the trap of actually thinking that introverts are weird. But this is because introverts believe there is more to life than the things only our senses can pick up. They acknowledge the fact that mushy, pink powerhouse pulsing in our skulls is capable of growing cities, create helpful inventions and devise ways to end the world's most pressing problems. They know what human beings are capable of with just the right amount of time to think things through.

An introvert is also someone who keeps to himself, only because he finds no desire to discuss trivialities.

He wants to reserve his talking for the things that truly matter. This is because he knows his priorities and he does not want to give away an idea that should take a lot of time to refine. His ability to grasp every word can only be trumped by the level of awkwardness with which he suffers in every social encounter.

Her silence speaks volumes about the machinery in her head. In a group, she is the one who speaks the least because she is mindful of the words people normally throw around. Her preciseness in the use of language and her ability to detect a bad idea if she hears one are a deadly combination, but she is subdued by a feeling of humiliation. She is almost reluctant to speak up for fear of being ostracized or branded as a know-it-all.

He is always the butt of jokes. Absent-minded and always the fall guy for every botched plan, he is at the receiving end of life's miseries, mostly because he lacks the amount of assertiveness required to get through every challenge. He is overwhelmed by people who take advantage of his subdued demeanor, perhaps too much that it becomes unbearable.

When she feels exploited, she will go extreme lengths to take care of business, and in the case of an introvert it simply means that she will address it using rational and not emotion. Left alone, she will work on something either too beautiful to ignore or too ingenuous to overlook. She is that smart.

But he is also a person who genuinely cares about the people around him. He does not express that because showing too much of an emotion is counterproductive to realizing long-term goals. Still, his love for his other-half, his family and his friends is equaled by his longing to be recognized for what he does. There is no truth in thinking that introverts know nothing about love, but they already know too much of what it means to love unconditionally.

Love happens to be one of the things that fuel her thirst to be creative. Her mind is as beautiful as a Diego Rivera mural. However, like the works of this great Mexican artist, she knows how to connect tiny bits of inspiration to make stories that mirror her life and the lives of others. Her aesthetic taste knows no bounds because she knows what beauty consists of. She knows her Shakespeare and is always bound to a feeling of liberation. She sees the arts as an endless sea of inspiration rather than a dull freeway lined with billboards of overrated celebrities and mundane taglines.

In every endeavor, an introvert is a special person who is not bound to a single concept. An introvert is more of an analytical machine, capable of discerning the inner workings of the mind, making great assumptions that can benefit the future, and taking care of his emotions while preventing them from fomenting a coup d'état against reason.

Who's Who in the World of Introversion

To put it all in a nut shell, an introvert is someone who knows how to handle the most powerful weapons man has ever possessed: the brain. It also makes perfect sense that the world's smartest people have been the most detached.

Albert Einstein for instance, has been known to be peculiar among his peers because he dressed differently. Unbeknownst to them, Einstein was only hiding his true prowess, which manifested later on when he published his theory of relativity which would become a driving force in the study of physics and energy.

The writer Franz Kafka was also known to possess strange habits. A man who mostly prefers to be alone rather than enjoy life outside his dreary job, Kafka wrote several novels about desolation and uncertainty that have impacted literature as well as other art forms for decades.

The philosopher Immanuel Kant was also a man who was proud to be an introvert, and he was good at it too! Every day, he spent his time in deep contemplation about the most ethical means by which men should act. He was too serious with this endeavor that he spends monotonous days following a schedule that left very little room for socialization.

But his influence on modern metaphysics and ethics can never be denied.

We can also include tech giants like Bill Gates and Mark Zuckerberg into the fold of course. Both men have become big names in the world of computing and entrepreneurship, and this is mainly because they used their inward abilities to innovate what were once unassuming ideas into the two greatest brands the world has ever known: Microsoft and Facebook.

Bill Gates

Success is not often the result of chance. For some people, taking chances is like taking on a raging bull head on. You do not really care about the result. You only care about how it will influence you. In other words, taking chances does not always mean we will gain something good from them. It only means that we are mature enough to take risks.

That is the case with Bill Gates who, introverted as he is, created a software company that has supplied countless businesses with computing solutions. He also created one of the world's leading manufacturers of software, making life easier not only for many business owners, but the common users as well.

How did he pull it off? Well, he maintained close focus on what is needed to be done. He did not waste his time with other activities. Although, he also found time for other things, he never failed to use his intellectual prowess to make something out of the limited capital he owned.

William Henry Gates III was known to be a smart kid growing up in Seattle, Washington. He was not like the other kids. While they were busy getting interested by the new toys of his day, he set his eyes on a subject no one thought would be appropriate for a young lad. He was familiar with programming at a very young age and took interest in building codes for machines. He had a fascination for how machines can have the ability to think, which was a totally abstract thing only humans are capable of doing. Eventually, this fascination turned into a lifelong interest in building computer solutions for many big companies.

By the time he graduated from high school, he scored high at an aptitude test and was accepted at Harvard in 1973, enrolling as a pre-law student. Even though he enrolled in a different course, he managed to get his brain to work rigorously as he took complex math and computing subjects.

At Harvard, his interest for computers only grew. His intellectual ability became more of a feature, and rather than focus on graduating from the college, he chose to pursue his passion for computers. Eventually, he dropped out of college and his parents understood him. It was not like he was throwing his future away. He just felt like there are more worthwhile things out there which can give him the kind of happiness he was yearning.

So what can we learn from Bill Gates attitude at school? That being lazy assures success? Absolutely not. Gates taught us to appreciate what we have. And while graduating from a very famous college is something one should strive for, it is the fact that there are goals out there that are far more worthwhile. Gates showed us how a true blue introvert operates. An introvert is not concerned with attaining a certain end. He is far more concerned about what he is going to do with the free time and creativity he has. For Gates, what was important to him was to satiate his need to learn more about a certain concept, master it, and use it as his ladder towards success. This is not to disparage school in any way, but it makes a perfect case for introverts to pursue their interests whatever it takes.

Like Gates, introverts get bored easily and all too often, they tend to give up on things that are superficial to them. In a way, they are very mindful of their own interests. If they lost a yearning for something, they will always have something in mind to pursue, a sort of "spare goal" to achieve. Aside from that, Gates showed us how curiosity can always bring a whole lot of benefits to an introvert. Naturally inquisitive, an introvert will never cease to amaze himself by researching about a particular concept and always finding ways on how to recreate it in their minds. Gates was able to nourish and grow his love for computers when he became fascinated by how they are programmed to do certain functions. He wanted to replicate the operations behind programming, and so he spent a lot of time perfecting his craft: programming. From then on, he continued to gain more knowledge about his field, which convinced him to love it even more.

So, whatever happened to Bill Gates? Well, eventually he hooked up with some friends developed an interpret which laid the groundwork for software giant Microsoft. Gates never went back to Harvard again, except of course for numerous occasions he was invited to speak and share his success story to other aspiring innovators.

You see, being an introvert does not give you a bad rap for being lazy. It is just that your mind is set on things that might not interest some people, but you they are part of an even bigger aspiration. From trying to mimic the code of a simple computer to building a software empire no office space can live without, Gates has truly showed the world what it means to be an introvert, how to use one's mind in creating something beautiful.

Is there something we can learn from Bill Gates? There is actually, and that is the value of hard work and brainpower. Having a curious mind is never a curse. It is a blessing and it is one blessing that can invoke an innovator in everyone.

Mark Zuckerberg

What's with introverts and technology?

One thing is for sure, technology is that realm of specialization where an introverts powers of problem solving and creative thinking come into play. For the most part, introverts love solving problems, and they can never settle for anything less than practical reasoning to create useful systems.

Aside from Bill Gates, many more from the tech industry have made a name for themselves. And it is correct to assume that most of these bad boys and girls considered themselves outcasts who view the world through different eyes.

And just like Bill Gates, Mark Zuckerberg culled success from using all the time he had to create a website that would soon take the internet by storm. And just like gates, Zuckerberg got his success by focusing intensively on his goals. The fame and success he claimed was never an accident. It was his sheer determination and his own curiosity that propelled him to become better and brighter.

But how can an introvert like him created something as omnipotent as Facebook?

Well, just like any other success story, we begin by observing his beginnings as a child. Growing up with a dentist cum computer whiz as a father, Mark developed an inkling for computers. It was through this nurturing that Mark discovered his real interest in developing software tools and games. Using his introverted nature, he spent his study learning as much as he can about programming and developing web tools. The internet was not much a significant part of people's lives back then as it is now, but it was in this backdrop of the information age that Mark continually updated his skills to fit the ever changing technological environment of his time. Eventually, Mark developed a messaging service for his father's clinic. This service would later influence the development of messaging software.

At school, Mark was never always the geek that many people today see him. He was active in sports and had close friends who would spend time with him doing wacky stuff. But it was when alone that Mark became a very formidable mind. At Harvard, he was able to develop a program which became the precursor to Facebook. Using his intuitiveness and creativity, Mark created FaceSmash as a way for Harvard students to rank other students based on their "hotness." It became a popular tool and everyone was in on it, creating a phenomenon that would also define the prevalence of the social media age. Eventually, Harvard shut FaceSmash down, but Mark did not let up. Instead, he picked up from the success of FaceSmash and developed an even better idea, of course with the help of some business-minded people.

The original idea was for Mark to create a social networking service called HarvardConnection.com. We all know how they ended up in the long run from *The Social Network*. Problems who gets to keep what percentage of Facebook ruptured Mark's relationship with the very people who had been there from the very beginning.

Whether or not Facebook's birth was the result of plagiarism is beyond us. What we do know is that Mark took a step forward in creating something that is truly magnificent. After all, he was the one who was building the code for the website. And he believed he can make something much better than what his partners had previously advocated.

When Facebook was finally launched in 2004, other universities from across the United States wanted in on the action. Eventually the idea spread and became even more popular as more and more people signed up for an account.

At present, Mark Zuckerberg is one of the world's richest people, with billions of individuals connected in a wide network where personal connectivity is the prime motivation.

So what can we learn from the Zuck?

Well, there is controversy in the way he became the prime architect of the social media world. And it was because he acted on his passion. When you say you are an introvert, it is not something to be ashamed of. Rather, to become an introvert is actually a privilege you can never obtain from anywhere else. As we can already know from Gates and Zuckerberg, there are infinite possibilities for people – even introverts like them – to achieve great successes.

It is only a matter of knowing how to be a great individual and how to start acting like one. There is not set formula for success that introverted people should follow. You only need to make one big leap ahead. For Mark, it only came as a blessing when his father taught him how to code. Eventually, this first exposure developed into a willingness to explore the world of computing. It also nourished the intellectual gifts he had by giving new and complex challenges.

Introverts have the gift of the mind, and they will never – not even once – spend time on something they know wouldn't pass off as an opportunity to learn. As an introvert, you need to understand that your mind is made for logic. It is made for rigorous thinking and allowing it to idle most of the time wouldn't really help you achieve its prime purpose. All you need to do is to discover your passions and learn from the fact that you are capable of making rich ideas that can benefit a lot of people.

In this case, you will need to do better each day. It is hard for an introvert like you, what with your penchant for procrastination and not getting things done. But really, you only need to find something that interests you and expound on it. Do more than what your healthy mind can do. Make your time count. Even if it seems like an impossible thing to do, you need to do it, because you are simply born to do it. Nothing else can explain that beautiful mind of yours. If Gates and Zuckerberg were able to use their heads in impacting the world, then you can do it too.

You just need to find that little spark that will push you towards achieving anything your heart desires.

There are many ways to describe introverts and their introversion, but it is always worth noting that whatever introverts do, they are doing it competently. Knowing the great contributions introverts have made over recent history should be enough to tell us that they are a special lot, maybe the type of people that humanity needs.

They have wellsprings of inspiration within them, and the one thing they should do is to tap into them and bring out their greatest strengths. Maybe someday, you can be put in a book like this to push other introverts towards realizing their own goals.

Chapter 2. Meditation: Will Power through Mind Power

We can all agree that introverts are basically inward-looking creatures basically disinterested with the mundane things happening outside their heads.

So, it is important to point out that introverts draw a bulk of their power from within. That in turn, becomes their major selling point when it comes to confronting a wide range of tasks and issues.

Introverts have it easy in a manner of speaking, seeing that all of them are able to think things through clearer lenses than most people. On the other hand, this ability is often overshadowed by their reluctance to share anything their twisted minds can think of.

It is for this reason that introverts are a special lot. Because they are silent most of the time, often taking up an unassuming stance to direct attention elsewhere in a bid to guard what they are most capable of doing.

However, some introverts seem to struggle with the idea of using one's inner strengths. This is partly due to the fact that concentration has always been a challenge, especially among people who prefer tranquil places in the form of remote Buddhist monasteries for example.

Meditation works only if you are in the right kinds of places. But this is just a promotion to force you to book a flight to Nepal or the Himalayas. Unknown to them is the fact that anywhere can become the right place for self-reflection.

How do you do it? It's just a matter of looking into these nifty tricks for turning your mind into your own personal cerebral temple.

Know when to cool off

For meditation to work, you first need to relax your mind and free it of any harmful thought. That may sound rather far-fetched and difficult, but attaining that initial feeling of tranquility is essential to make you feel more at home in your head.

Every day, we are faced with countless problems and issues that affect our decision-making and critical thinking processes. Especially for people who work in highly technical occupations requiring immense brain power, stress can put one down like a boot puts down an ant. Superior as they seem in terms of intellectual energy, introverts also need some time to recharge their super-computer like heads. They process information to such a degree that relaxation becomes something more like a luxury for them. They need to cool down, and when they feel this need creeping up to them and affecting their work, they know how to push themselves away from the desk and put their minds in hibernation mode, and that creates the right condition for meditation.

Stress takes a heavy toll on an introvert's head, so it does help to just turn off for some time, recede into one's secure place and be comfortable with the momentary silence.

Do you hear that? Crickets. Your brain is silent for now. Take this time to breathe in and breathe out.

Breathing

When you feel anxious, you breathe deeply and let all that fear out in one resonating sigh. If you feel so stressed about work and just want to be in the comfort of your head, breathe in all the positive energy and breathe out the negative.

It sounds so cliché, but it works. Stress and anxiety causes us to panic, diminishing our ability to think. But if we decide to compose ourselves through one big breath, we are able to clearly identify problems and resolve them.

Introverts are over thinkers. Seeing that they are so insightful, they often explore the possibility a certain problem would go out of hand, creating more complex problems in the long run. This is one weakness that introverts have, but it is something a deep breath can cure.

So before you sink into the depths of that wonderful head of yours, try to release the problems in one deep and solid breath. You will need that in order to find your happy place.

Finding your Happy Place

Everyone has a happy place; that area in your mind where you feel so secured, where everything goes the way you wanted. Introverts of course are no exception. They have a happy place in their heads and by god, these are the best castles one can see. By going to your happy place, you are able to make sense of our thoughts and make you more attuned with the problem you are facing.

So, as an introvert, what should your happy place look like?

Well, we are dealing with abstract concepts here, but finding your happy place should not lead you far. It is always there, and it needs you to be there also. Whether it's a garden filled with lush, collector's ferns or a Star Trek convention where everyone dresses up like Spock. Happiness is relative, and an introvert has a treasure trove of sources from which he or she can become happy. Once you are happy, your ability to comprehend complex concepts become even more powerful.

Find your Motivation

What drives you?

That's from a car commercial (I think). Nevertheless, the fact remains that introverts do not necessarily do the kind of work they do just because they like doing it. No! It is because there is a motivating factor in every single project they get their hands on, and once that becomes clear, they will use this motivation to multiply their skills and abilities even more.

Whether it be a promotion or a scholarship grant to a major university, anything can be achieved once we have something that pushes us to take the leap.

Going Back to Reality

This kind of meditation aims to improve the way you handle things in spite of a mental burnout. Once you master these tips, there is nothing else you can do except to seize the day with a more apt mind.

Chapter 3. Unleashing your strengths

If you choose to make your life a lot easier as an introvert, you may as well practice and apply a few things. Meditation does not always cut it, and sometimes you may want extra help with everyday challenges.

Listen closely to what others say

Introverts are usually branded as absent-minded daydreamers that do not know what is going on around them. This is because they feed on acquired information the way a wine connoisseur samples a Merlot. Truth be told, introverts are often the poorest listeners. In that case, it is essential for an introvert to exercise better listening. Take time to listen to the radio (since radio broadcasts are uninterrupted by "Wait, I didn't catch that) and try to analyze the words you picked up.

Get a little confidence boost

Apparently, introverts are not the best communicators. As much as we want them to admit it, introverts seem to have a dearth in forging interpersonal relationships solely because they lack a socializing function in them. Because of this lack, they seem to communicate less confidently than others. One way to solve this is by TALKING WITH PEOPLE. There's nothing much to it other than to engage in real-world conversations with other people. Does it sound difficult? Well, it does at first, but it gets easier every day. Practicing conversations on topics as simple as the weather can stimulate your socialization skills and allow you to become better at conversing with other people. If at first you are reluctant, you can always have someone right beside you to act as your talking buddy. Start with simple topics and work your way up to bigger and more complex issues. You would be surprised how much of an interesting person you would be to yourself and each another.

Go on solitary walks

Great minds work well when left alone. But when walking, they develop a lot of beautiful ideas. There is a sort of therapeutic characteristic of taking walks in the park or around the house. Not only is it great exercise, but some introverts find something meaningful out of taking casual, solitary walks. It's slower and you enjoy the hustle and bustle of nature with every step. You are taking all of it in, giving yourself a good view at how life should be enjoyed: slow and steady.

During your days off, might I suggest turning off the PC, going outside and setting your mobile phone to instrumental jazz music. You would feel more calm and relaxed and happier seeing that the mood keeps you afloat from all the stress.

Plan your day ahead

Introverts are normally guilty of being unorganized and it is because of this that they tend to miss important deadlines and lose sight of small but important objects (think about the keys you left on the pantry, you absent-minded fool!). Apparently, this is one weakness that puts introverts at a great disadvantage, but this is one simple issue that can always be resolved by having a planner. Now, we are not ostracizing you for your inability to perceive time as it ticks by, but at least a planner allows you to be more in tune with important dates for turning in output.

In some way, planners help you to stick to a schedule, another activity most introverts are not good at. It's a matter of discipline really, and it is also about keeping your main priorities intact. Introverts are known for their indifference towards these conventions, but there are still those who are able to deliver in time and who still know where they put their keys.

The fact of the matter is that introverts have a bad sense of keeping a schedule, but it is something that is actually practiced every day – just like talking to random strangers for instance.

Take responsibility

Let's go back to one weakness an introvert is notoriously known for. Being unorganized creatures, people who are looking within, are unaware of every result that was sourced from their actions. In some way, introverts have a lack of regard for taking responsibility, and it comes with the fact that they would rather blame other people for their mistakes. We are not talking generally here, but there are cases when one doesn't feel like taking the brunt of a problem and asking others to be sacrificial lambs, and this is one quality that alienates introverts in the first place.

Egos can take the place of reason, and that is where the fatal flaw of being a lone wolf lies. As a result, people are turned off by your actions and dismiss you as another know-it-all trying to prove himself. This affects professional relationships as much as it obstructs you from functioning in pursuit of personal and organizational goals. At any rate, you may want to take the safe route by taking responsibility for whatever issue arises, as long as it relates to the nature of your work. I know it is hard to accept responsibility, but being people whose minds are more fixated towards reason, the best things you can do is to set your ego aside and take responsibility. Admit your mistakes and silently work your way towards redeeming yourself. Not many people can do it, so to see an introvert actually having the guts to admit a mistake, is something you won't see every day.

Take control of your mind

Now we come to the most important part of being an introvert: Having to manage that engine of a brain!

This is not to say that introverts are robots in their own peculiar way, but it says a lot about how much dilemma they encounter on a daily basis, starting with how to effectively control their heads.

Imaginative and innovative. These are two words that best describe an introvert. Yet these only serve to cover up a deeper struggle. Introverts have to battle themselves in order to open up to other people. They have within them a sort of goblin of sorts that does not allow free rein of one's thoughts.

Luckily, once an introvert takes control of this goblin, he is able to take control of how he deals with the outside world. For a start, that goblin is the reason why you are always reluctant to go out of the house and mingle with other people and it is also the reason why you put off any work. It suppresses your industrious side in favor of your lazier side.

So what should you do about it? Well, just ignore it. It doesn't do much good to keep it inside and it doesn't help to give it control over your life decisions either. Always remember that your life is what you make of it. You always have the choice of letting the goblin run your life, or free yourself from its control and take the high road towards success.

As reasonable as you are, you would probably pick the option that would give your life a whole lot of meaning.

Keep a journal

Living as an introvert can be difficult. You might have realized this earlier in this book, but it is true that introverts have it more difficult than most people. What with the loneliness and the constant struggle to socialize (even if you lack an understanding thereof), there is really much work before introverts can truly unleash the full capacity of their powers.

The road towards success for an introvert is one that takes several steps. It is also a journey filled with drama. So, we can say a lot about the maelstrom of emotions prevailing in an introvert's quest for self-realization. Come to think of it, it makes for a great deal of interesting content.

Keeping journals and recording your life's progress has some sort of therapeutic effect all on its own. For one, it's a great way for silent, inexpressive people to vent out their frustrations. It also a great way to acquire inspiration for a book or a painting.

For some reason, keeping journals have not lost its appeal to many young people. Social media is already there for us to indulge in. Apparently, there is a difference between showing off for the sake of validation, and actually recording the most important scenes of your life for personal progress.

We all see how introverts struggle with the fact that they are alone and that they have peculiar qualities that no one else understands. However, if provided with ample time, they will be able to use these very same qualities to their advantage by channeling energies to become more productive and positive,

you might as well be closer towards attaining the
goals that you set for yourself.

Chapter 4. Goals for Lone Wolves

There is a saying that "no man is an island" and introverts seem to live by this mantra. In everything they do, they believe they are the only ones who can do it correctly.

While it has its perks, the aloofness that comes with being an introvert incites negative impressions among friends, family and colleagues. Introverts are so enamored by their ability to work alone that they tend to shun assistance of any form. They have a sense of responsibility they think their isolation from outside forces can maintain.

At the same time, this forces people to back away from an introvert when he or she is carried away by work. In extreme cases, people tend to think lone wolves are egotistical maniacs who do not listen to advice and are so sure of themselves not to let others take the reins.

This is unavoidable. It is in the nature of introverts to have extreme levels of trust in themselves and have little or no regard for group dynamics. Needless to say, one can always see beauty of some form from this end.

Ideas are generated endlessly in a lone wolf's head. But the only problem is that he or she is unwilling to share even bits of these ideas to anyone else, for fear of being ostracized and getting unwanted attention. On the other hand, introverts are mainly theoretical creatures that feed only on abstract thinking and, in terms of application, seem reluctant to take the first step.

A lone wolf lifestyle is one that is exciting. Think about all of the quiet and unassuming personalities that built business empires out of sheer creativity. Introverts have all the powers they can get when they know it has a liberating characteristic, but it requires just as much will power to actually harness the grand abilities of a silent worker.

So, lone wolves, listen up. Here's how you can use your isolated and detached personalities to get things done.

Make time for planning

For introverts, this is similar to a walk in the park. They practically do not have any problem coming up with strategies and techniques to approach a problem. But in many cases, this is something that should be worked out, since introverts are notoriously known for being procrastinators who put off every opportunity to finish a job as soon as possible.

When you are faced with a project you know is valuable for personal and professional development, do not spare any time daydreaming about the results. Go for the shovel and start digging for important ideas to get you started. You would not waste any time as well as energy as you think things through.

Manage you time

Let me repeat what I wrote earlier: "INTROVERTS ARE NOTORIOUSLY KNOWN FOR BEING PROCRASTINATORS."

Enough said. Well, on the contrary, I did not say enough so let me just show you how important it is to manage your time. Lone wolves are, in all respects, individuals who value freedom from constraints of any form, and that includes time. Because of overconfidence, sometimes deadlines are not met. People with such an inclination towards shunning conventionality tend to deconstruct the rationale behind deadlines. Simultaneously, they often undervalue the importance of a timetable to other people (clients and professors who expect them to turn in their work, for example).

Therefore, introverts should keep their confidence in check and actually adhere to a well-organized timetable. They have all the brain power they need to provide good quality work and lead amazing lives. But imagine them managing their time wisely to prepare for whatever may come.

Brainstorm... with other people

You mean, socializing?! GASP!

It's a real shocker but hey, when you work for an organization or you're just planning a personal project on your own, it would seem like a good idea to momentarily leave our shells and talk about what others are thinking. You would probably object to the notion of talking even if you are not up for it. But what is fascinating about introverts is that they are dedicated to a goal, to a point that they lose some semblance of their aloofness in order to collaborate and engage in discussions that also enrich themselves.

So when it comes down to actual planning, it would actually benefit you in terms of materializing whatever comes to your head. Every organization is blessed with its own ragtag team of prodigies who, if afforded the appropriate avenue for nourishment, would churn out quality work that everyone can enjoy. So in the end, wolves still need a pack for survival.

Take some time to critique

One advantage of being an introvert is you are able to see things from several perspectives. It is because of this ability to be insightful that lone wolves, in spite of their detached nature, are apparently more cognizant of defects.

What's more, being aloof means you are able to focus on the things that should improve something. You should also be able to attain a clearer grasp of the objectives you need to accomplish as a unit in a group. But it takes guts, really. Introverts tend to lose a fervor for critiquing if it means having to share one's observations with others. Still, you can get around by participating in meetings where everything is open for discussion. Criticisms are always welcome and it doesn't help if your reluctance to decide which course or project should override personal and group goals.

Apparently, we can all say that these tips for lone wolves apply only in the work place. B introverts exist in other places as well, and it is essential to know about how well you can create original plans and strategies. You have the gift of self-reliance, but it is also the same gift that makes you valuable as an employee or student or whatever.

So when you think lone wolves are cool, you are right! Because they know how to take control of their intellect and channel most of their energies towards the greater good.

Chapter 5. Let your Creativity Flourish

Another selling point of being an introvert is that you are able to express whatever is currently in your head. Most introverts are known to wield the powers of an artisan, one who is able to create magnificent works of art. We are not really talking about just the visual arts, but we are also delving into the spheres of music, sculpture and literature.

As evidenced by the output of such individuals as Picasso and Stephen King, introverts do possess an inclination towards beautiful and meaningful things.

Consider yourself lucky when you count as one among countless of talented stars that shine bright in the artistic universe. Because you are able to see inside the ideas that you nurture in your head, you are also able to wield just about the right amount of clarity to empty out your brain and produce truly magnificent works of art.

Want to bring out the creative in you? Here are some important ways to go about it.

Make room for hobbies

Introverts tend to be looked upon as isolated individuals with peculiar tastes in terms of seeking fun and excitement. We are also made to believe that introverts care little about free time. It isn't so, since most introverts prefer to spend idle time on interests considered boring among the more snobbish extroverts.

Hobbies play a major role in stimulating introverts' curiosity. Usually, they spend significant amounts of time solving puzzles like Sudoku, or engage in highly entertaining online games. There are also those who tend to burn a little time by writing poems, sketching and photography. Introverts always have an eye for the beautiful as much as they have an eye for things with organic or inorganic meaning, and this is the kind of stimulation that introverts truly enjoy.

You might want to bring a sketchpad outside and draw whatever the scenery provides. During rainy days, you might try to cordon yourself in the bedroom and listen to the sound of droplets inviting you to write a poem about them. Or if you are up for a little adventure, go hiking up a hill or mountain you always wanted to conquer, reach the peak and take a snapshot of the vast view that will last a lifetime.

There is inspiration everywhere and it makes perfect for an introvert to use his ability to absorb his surroundings and produce a replication of what he finds as beautiful.

Spend time with creative people

One thing's for sure, as an introvert, you basically shun any form of socialization even if it means being inspired by it. Well, it does sound a good idea when you choose the kind of people you want to be with.

It's not that I am teaching you how to discriminate people based on their Myers-Briggs personality test results. But there is some truth to the saying that "birds of a feather, flock together." Therefore, there's nothing to lose when you start to talk with like-minded people. Rubbing elbows with the right personalities enables you to open up new galaxies of inspiration. You are able to exchange ideas, absorb new knowledge and apply new concepts to the things that interest you.

Go on cultural excursions

Here, you don't necessarily go on casual trips to the museum during the weekend. What this entails is to go wherever there is culture. Whether you plan on going on a trip to some remote village or attend a music festival featuring Australian Aboriginal folk music, the world is basically your oyster for cultural awareness.

Being open to other cultures allows you to open up your creative mind. It also gives you an opportunity to learn new things that your knowledge hungry mind wants to bite into. So if you know some sort of cultural event in your community, do not hesitate to join in and discover just how much there is to know about the world. Besides, you diary needs some interesting content to satiate its pages.

Make stories out of the everyday

What's the best thing about being an introvert? Well, you are as observant as a super detective. You tend to have this ability to assess people based on the way they dress, speak and walk. It's a gift. Though not exactly mutant in nature, but introverts are just so detail-oriented that they are able to generate intricate backstories for the people they see in the park for example. Which is why introverts make for the best writers – they are so interested in people that they choose to be on the sidelines and make up interesting stories.

Writing has its perks here, so as an introvert, you better convince yourself to publish a novel based on the people you meet. Not that it should mirror real-life, but at least it gives a semblance of people are rendered through your own unique perspective. For Jack Kerouac, sketching the lives of people is in itself a service to the arts. You are practically replicating what you see onto your own little canvas.

There are as many stories as there are people, and in case you take the literary route, might I suggest starting at a café? Order your favorite brew, sit down, and observe the people that are casually having their espressos with their cheesy conversations. You will surprised by how much material it entails to fill a 400-page novel!

Be inspired everyday

It might sound like a long shot, but inspiration as we know it is found everywhere. It's only a matter of going to where it usually settles. On the other hand, it's something more of a hit-or-miss endeavor. You do not exactly know where inspiration rests, but there is a good chance you would encounter it. Call it luck, but people have better odds when they start to take action.

Instead of lazing around all day, browsing memes, try to discover the good things about being an introvert by actually looking for inspiration instead of waiting for it to come. A successful man is one who believes in action and shuns illusions after all.

In essence, being an introvert is actually more about being a creative individual. Invoking the creativity in you won't be farfetched, just as long as you lead an authentic life that lives and breathes art.

Chapter 6. Be your Own Hero

Everyone has a hero because everyone needs to be inspired in some way. Fortunately for introverts, they shouldn't look far to find the right people to inspire them.

In all seriousness though, having a personal hero does have its cons. We tend to follow what another person does rather than become our authentic selves. It doesn't add up when introverts have an icon to follow, but at least they gain inspiration and insightful life lessons from the struggles of important introverted personalities.

It's really a healthy thing to have a hero, but at the end of the day, you are alone to settle your own dilemmas and put your inner demons to sleep. That can be a wonderful thing because introverts, when left alone, would actually work towards solving their own issues. They do not settle with the illusion of a superhero that will come to save them. They are more certain that their own ingenuity and cleverness will get them through the day.

In the end, no Batman will come to your rescue, but it becomes clear that a Bruce Wayne has been living inside your head and your heart all this time. You are eventually hit by the fact that you are your own hero, willing to save himself from whatever comes your way.

You have everything that makes you that special and that is one superpower no one will ever take away from you. With that, you might as well be a hero to somebody else. By using your introverted powers to do good, you can at least dismiss the idea that introverts are more likely to become mad scientists than protagonists in a comic book.

Conclusion

That ends our little presentation about the beauty of being introverted – or rather, the ways on how introverts can channel their energies towards realizing personal goals.

Thank you for purchasing this book and I hope you have learned as much as you have already understood that being introverted doesn't mean you are an outcast in some way. But rather, it is something of a gift that has to be constantly nurtured. Introverts have a potential for greatness and it's only a matter of bringing out this greatness so introverts can truly get more out of their lives.

If you are an introvert that has read this book all to the end, then I am thankful that you have taken the time to know just how much you are capable of. Just remember that there is no shame at preferring to spend your Saturday evening binge watching Game of Thrones or having LAN parties with friends you knew from college. The stuff you hear about introverts aren't necessarily true. And as you have read in this book, there is actually more to you than what meets the eye.

Again, I couldn't thank you enough for purchasing this book. I sure hope you will use what you have learned to make positive changes in your life that will make it a (surprisingly) more exciting one.

Here's to the silent lot!

Kenny Matthews